Learning with Findus and Pettson

Letters and Words

Everything starts with C

Findus is learning to spell and has been given a task by Pettson. Can you help him find and circle all the things that start with C?

Which path leads to Pettson?

Findus is lost on the farm and misses Pettson.
Which path should he choose to find his friend?

A   B   C

Find the letters

Can you help Findus find the right letters
to spell what is in the box?

M   N   O   G

E   H   T   V

A   R   K

_ _ _ _

Pack well

Pettson has offered to help Gustavsson fix the pig pen fence. Can you help him pack his tool bag? Circle the tools on Pettson's list.

SAW

TAPE MEASURE

WOOD

Which muckle?

Muckles are mischievous creatures who come in many different shapes and sizes. Can you find and circle the muckle described in the note?

PINK

IS POINTING

HAS A BAG

Which letter is missing?

The muckle has lost some letters from the words below. Can you help him work out which letters are missing?

T_ EE

P__CTURE

LO_K

What is where?

The hens have collected four things.
Do you know what these things are called?
Write the correct letter in the small box.

A = PIZZA   C = BIRD

B = CAR   D = VIOLIN

Secret muckle code

The muckles sometimes get annoyed because Findus can understand what they are saying, so they made a secret code. Can you work out what the muckles have written here?

 = A    = T    = C

= N   = H    = E

= F   = K   = B

What starts with S?

The hens need your help to find and circle all the things that start with the letter in the box.

Word search

Findus has hidden words in this letter grid.
What words can you find?
You can search ➡ horizontally and ⬇ vertically.

CAR	CAKE	FUN
CAT	FISH	ROSE
TEA	SHED	TOY

F	I	S	H	E	M	T	O	Y	I
Z	S	C	U	V	P	L	R	N	G
S	R	D	H	I	R	E	C	P	A
H	I	C	A	R	O	Q	A	K	U
E	G	N	P	Z	Y	A	T	Q	W
D	T	U	S	C	A	L	I	B	I
S	E	I	M	A	P	N	A	I	F
O	B	U	R	K	E	R	N	W	U
T	E	A	K	E	N	U	K	A	N
E	W	N	O	P	R	O	S	E	D

Who likes what?

Can you draw lines between the pictures in the 2 rows so that everyone gets what they like best?

Something beginning with B

The painter muckle is supposed to paint
something that starts with the letter B,
but she can't think of anything.
Can you help her?

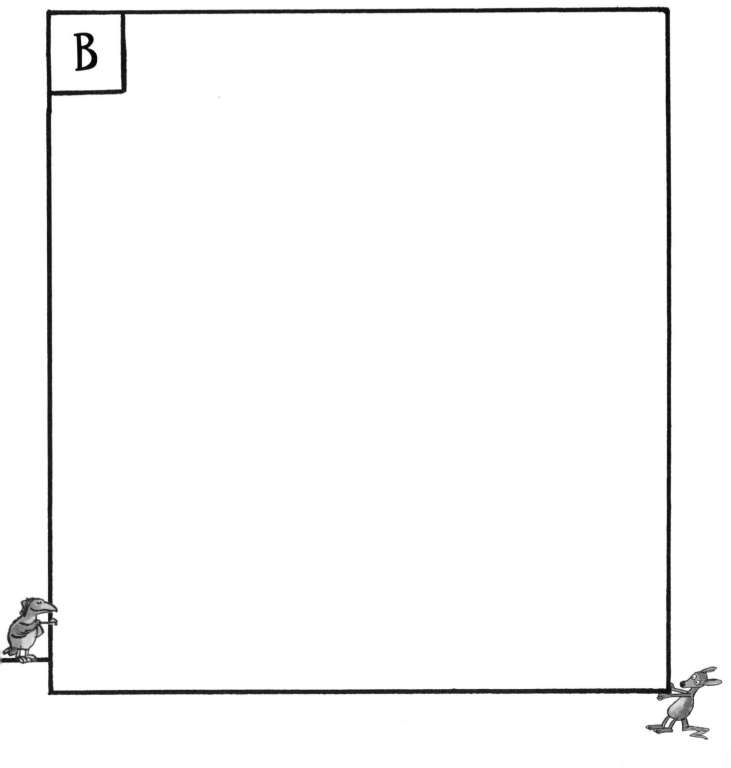

Letter maze

The muckles want to go home but
they can only cross the grid by
stepping on the letter R.
Can you show them the right path?

R	R	A	B	K	W	J	I	P	S
A	R	R	R	R	E	P	O	Z	K
O	E	D	I	R	R	C	A	T	B
T	H	Y	O	U	R	S	H	M	F
Q	V	N	P	A	R	R	G	U	N
J	E	C	P	U	Y	R	R	I	A
I	X	M	L	D	U	X	R	Y	B
D	H	F	T	F	O	R	R	Z	C
S	U	T	F	G	J	R	A	D	E
A	Z	A	H	H	B	R	R	R	R

Mixed up words

The cheeky muckles have confused Pettson by mixing up the letters. Can you put them in the right order?

OHSE = ___ ___ ___ ___

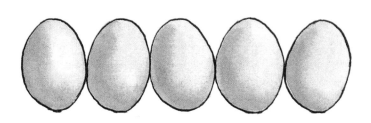

GESG = ___ ___ ___ ___

Prillan's things

Prillan the hen is looking for things that start with the letter P, like her name. Can you help her?

Who lives where?

Findus chased a hen that was chasing a muckle and now everyone is lost! Can you show them the way back to their homes?

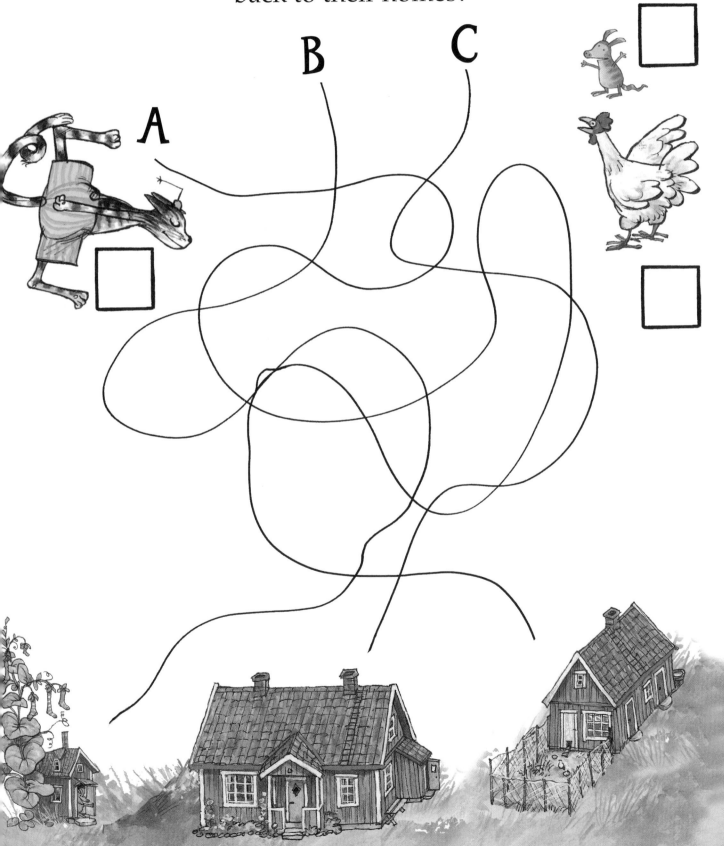

Word search

Findus has hidden his words again.
What words can you find this time?
You can search ➡ horizontally and ⬇ vertically.

CARROT	SUN	HEN
MUCKLE	FOOTBALL	FROG
JAM	MUSIC	

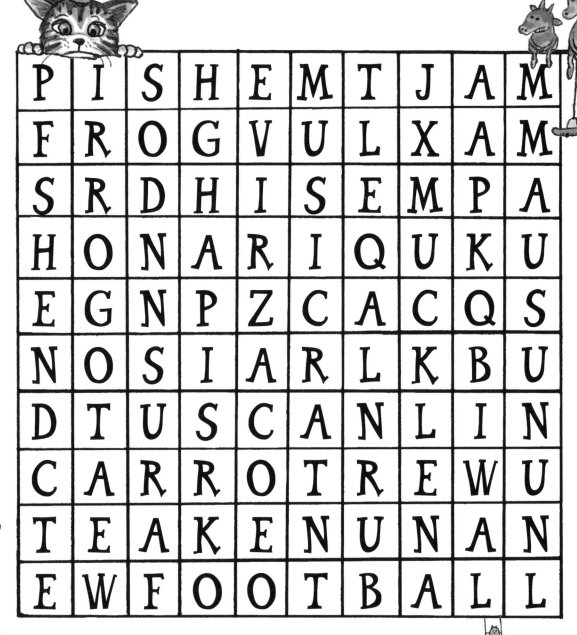

P	I	S	H	E	M	T	J	A	M
F	R	O	G	V	U	L	X	A	M
S	R	D	H	I	S	E	M	P	A
H	O	N	A	R	I	Q	U	K	U
E	G	N	P	Z	C	A	C	Q	S
N	O	S	I	A	R	L	K	B	U
D	T	U	S	C	A	N	L	I	N
C	A	R	R	O	T	R	E	W	U
T	E	A	K	E	N	U	N	A	N
E	W	F	O	O	T	B	A	L	L

Who am I?

Findus has found a note describing an animal
but he can't work out which it is.
Can you draw a circle round the right one?

ANGRY

FOUR LEGS

BLACK

What is the first letter?

Pettson has dragged some things from the shed and
asked Findus what letter they start with.
Can you help him?

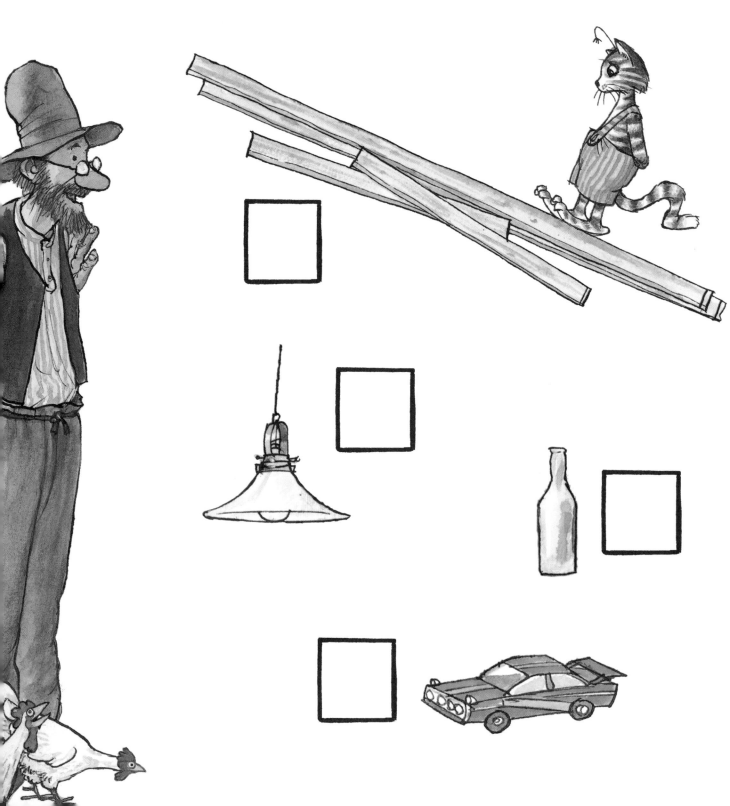

Something beginning with T

The painter muckle wants to paint something
again, this time beginning with T.
Can you help her?

T

Find the letters

Can you help Findus find the right letters
to spell what's in the box?

R   O   T

L   N   T   A

R   X   I

Y   S   H

_ _ _ _

Secret muckle code

The muckles have used their secret code again!
What have they written this time?

_____   _____   _____   _____   _____

= T   = R   = I

= V   = W   = P

= O   = E   = A

Mixed up words

The chickens have been arguing about how different words are spelled and now they are really confused. Can you help them unscramble the letters?

 **SEBKAT** =

— — — — — — —

 **EHECES** =

— — — — — — —

 **TORACR** =

— — — — — — —

Which letter is missing?

The muckle's friends have hidden some of the
letters she needs to spell the things below.
Can you add the missing letters?

JA_

B_G

C_TTON

FIS_

What does it start with?

Findus has got some things from the
kitchen and wants Pettson to tell
him what letter they start with.
Can you help?

Letter maze

The muckles show Findus their letter maze
and tell him he can only step on vowels to get
across the maze to the cake. Can he make it?

R	B	F	C	R	P	G	T	L	M
U	A	X	H	L	Z	W	B	R	G
D	I	W	M	F	C	Q	W	X	P
G	E	Y	E	I	A	L	M	H	W
C	A	O	U	D	I	Z	T	F	N
K	N	Z	W	V	A	U	S	Z	T
B	W	F	R	Q	C	O	G	J	C
F	P	D	H	W	X	E	A	I	Y
H	G	X	D	P	F	N	R	U	P
V	T	L	Q	Z	M	T	B	E	D

TIP!
Vowels = A, E, I, O, U

Secret muckle code

The muckles have written another secret message!
What does it say?

___ ___ ___   ___ ___ ___

 = E   = D   = N

= A   = K   = G

= H   = S   = T

The alphabet

A B C D E F G

H I J K L M N

O P Q R S T

U V W X Y Z

a b c d e f g h i

j k l m n o p q r

s t u v w x y z

Answers

Everything starts with C

Findus is learning to spell and has been given a task by Pettson. Can you help him find and circle all the things that start with C?

Which path leads to Pettson?

Findus is lost on the farm and misses Pettson. Which path should he choose to find his friend?

Find the letters

Can you help Findus find the right letters to spell what is in the box?

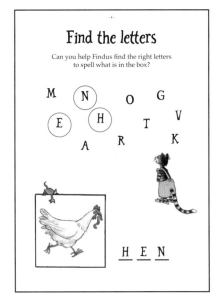

Pack well

Pettson has offered to help Gustavsson fix the pig pen fence. Can you help him pack his tool bag? Circle the tools on Pettson's list.

Which muckle?

Muckles are mischievous creatures who come in many different shapes and sizes. Can you find and circle the muckle described in the note?

Which letter is missing?

The muckle has lost some letters from the words below. Can you help him work out which letters are missing?

What is where?

The hens have collected four things. Do you know what these things are called? Write the correct letter in the small box.

Secret muckle code

The muckles sometimes get annoyed because Findus can understand what they are saying, so they made a secret code. Can you work out what the muckles have written here?

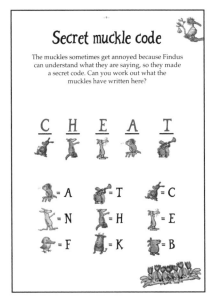

What starts with S?

The hens need your help to find and circle all the things that start with the letter in the box.

Answers

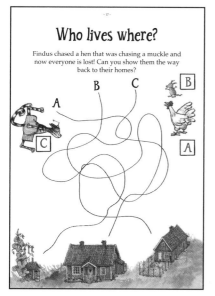

Answers

What is the first letter?

Pettson has dragged some things from the shed and asked Findus what letter they start with. Can you help him?

W
L
B
C

Something beginning with T

The painter muckle wants to paint something again, this time beginning with T. Can you help her?

Find the letters

Can you help Findus find the right letters to spell what's in the box?

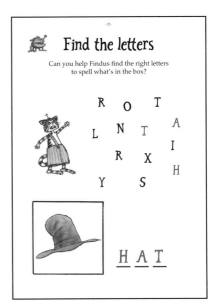

R O T
L N T A
R X I
Y S H

H A T

Secret muckle code

The muckles have used their secret code again! What have they written this time?

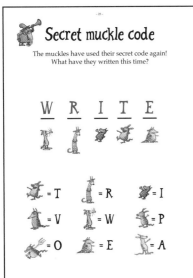

W R I T E

= T   = R   = I
= V   = W   = P
= O   = E   = A

Mixed up words

The chickens have been arguing about how different words are spelled and now they are really confused. Can you help them unscramble the letters?

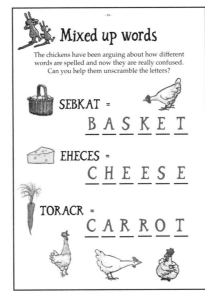

SEBKAT = B A S K E T

EHECES = C H E E S E

TORACR = C A R R O T

Which letter is missing?

The muckle's friends have hidden some of the letters she needs to spell the things below. Can you add the missing letters?

JA M

BA G

CO TTON

FIS H

What does it start with?

Findus has got some things from the kitchen and wants Pettson to tell him what letter they start with. Can you help?

S
R
O
E
B

Letter maze

The muckles show Findus their letter maze and tell him he can only step on vowels to get across the maze to the cake. Can he make it?

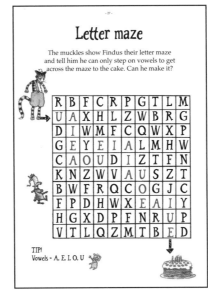

R	B	F	C	R	P	G	T	L	M
U	A	X	H	L	Z	W	B	R	G
D	I	W	M	F	C	Q	W	X	P
G	E	Y	E	I	A	L	M	H	W
C	A	O	U	D	I	Z	T	F	N
K	N	Z	W	V	A	U	S	Z	T
B	W	F	R	Q	C	O	G	J	C
F	P	D	H	W	X	E	A	I	Y
H	G	X	D	P	F	N	R	U	P
V	T	L	Q	Z	M	T	B	E	D

TIP!
Vowels = A, E, I, O, U

Secret muckle code

The muckles have written another secret message! What does it say?

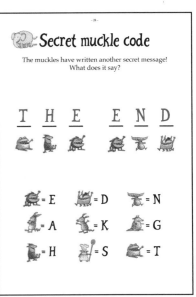

T H E   E N D

= E   = D   = N
= A   = K   = G
= H   = S   = T